Stay ⬚⬚⬚⬚⬚⬚ Healthy
While You Study

ABOUT THE AUTHOR

Financial wellbeing is critical to our mental and physical health. And financial education helps you understand how to make your money work better, empowering you with the confidence to thrive. It's the first step to financial health.

Former wealth manager **Vivi Friedgut** saw first-hand how financial knowledge impacts positive life outcomes. She is founder and CEO of Blackbullion, the award-winning startup transforming next-generation finances through financial education powered by technology. Vivi's on a mission to make sure everyone has access to financial wellbeing, driving inclusion, diversity and wellbeing.

A champion for the startup community, Vivi is an active media commentator and speaks passionately on financial literacy, entrepreneurship, resilience and the power of innovation.

Also available in this series:
Anxiety at University
Depression at University
Resourcefulness at University
Staying Well and Safe at University
Stay Calm While You Study
Stay Hopeful While You Study
Stay Safe While You Study
Stay Resilient While You Study
Stay Balanced While You Study
Stay Organized While You Study
Stay Happy While You Study

Stay Financially Healthy While You Study

Make the Most of Your Student Experience

VIVI FRIEDGUT

Published in 2023 by Trigger Publishing
An imprint of Shaw Callaghan Ltd
UK Office
The Stanley Building
7 Pancras Square
Kings Cross
London N1C 4AG

US Office
On Point Executive Center, Inc
3030 N Rocky Point Drive W
Suite 150
Tampa, FL 33607
www.triggerhub.org

A CIP catalogue record for this book is available upon request from the British Library
ISBN: 9781837963737
Ebook ISBN: 9781837963744

MIX
Paper from
responsible sources
FSC® C013056

To Zak, Ben, Mia, Sam, Tali and Ella.
None of you were born when I wrote the first book
but these months apart, while heartbreakingly hard,
gave me the space to write this one. There is
always a silver lining, though sometimes it's hard
to see, I hope you will always seek it out.
The future is yours to build...
so build it with passion.

CONTENTS

INTRODUCTION

When I first sat down to write this book I kept thinking of my own experience at uni. How daunting it was initially. Not the actual uni part of it, but all the bits around that. Would independence be exciting or terrifying? Would I be able to be accountable to myself with my study? Would I take responsibility for getting to 9am classes or would the snooze button be too alluring?

All beginnings are difficult, and every life milestone feels unique even though countless others have walked the path before and countless more will walk it afterwards. And while all of this is true, none of it matters because our journey is unique and in terms of higher education, the stakes are ever higher.

You are still far more likely to get a job as a graduate than a non-graduate, but the job market is getting tougher for everyone. While there remains a degree premium (meaning that you are likely to earn more as a graduate than you would without a degree), this has shrunk for most courses. And while there were always expenses associated with going to university, rarely have they been this high.

So much comes down to money. It impacts on everything, from what we eat to how much we can focus in class, to how well we feel and how well we sleep, and even how many clubs and societies we sign up to. How we handle money at uni will determine how long it will take us to build future wealth after graduation – whether we are building solid foundations or risking a downward spiral. Finance is the gateway – but the gateway to what is up to us.

And no one teaches this stuff. Understanding money is the one thing almost everyone agrees we should learn about much earlier than we do.

So, writing this book has been a labour of love for me to help prospective students develop good financial health to ease the way for everything else. And I wanted to address it head on. To avoid the fluff and nonsense, the lies and half-truths, and to present a clear line of sight toward the future and explain how decisions made at uni, and in preparing for uni, can have repercussions for a long time after graduation.

Stay Financially Healthy is more like a step-by-step guide, clearly pointing out the things you need to know but also why you need to know them and, most importantly, how to action them. We will delve into the journey from start to finish; what you should consider before starting uni as well as how to make the best of your money while you are there.

This book aims to help you:

- Understand how physical, mental and financial wellbeing are all connected
- Prepare holistically for going to uni
- Make your money work for you
- Deal with feelings of guilt, stress and anxiety
- Feel calm and in control of your finances
- Develop key financial skills for life

You'll find practical points of action so you can make decisions confident that you've taken the important factors into consideration. That's no guarantee you will make the right call every single time, but at least you'll know that your actions were considered, not impulsive.

Starting university can be daunting but it's the opportunity to think about who you want to be, figure out how to be the best version of yourself and take risks in a safe environment. As much as we'd like to, we can't protect you from everything, but we can help you get your mindset right and take care of your wellbeing, so that you can take confident steps toward the future knowing you can have control over your financial health, too.

CHAPTER 1

WHAT DOES IT MEAN TO BE FINANCIALLY HEALTHY?

If there is one critical piece of understanding I hope you get from reading this little book, it's that being aware of, paying attention to and boosting your financial health is critical to your overall wellbeing. In this first chapter, we will delve into the foundations of what that means and how you can relieve some of the pressure, mitigating some of your anxiety and concerns as a student. We'll examine what I call the "tripod of wellbeing", which places financial health firmly alongside mental and physical health in terms of importance in your life.

General mental health and wellbeing

For about a decade mental health has bubbled to the surface of the general consciousness. We have been told to protect our mental health, to guard ourselves from emotional upheaval and unhappiness – to be aware of our every emotion and to centre ourselves away from things that might cause us pain. Before delving into financial wellbeing to look at why it is the critical foundation beneath so much of our life, it is important to separate mental health from mental wellbeing.

The Mayo Clinic says that a mental health disorder may be present when patterns or changes in thinking, feeling or behaving cause distress or disrupt a person's ability to function. Those with a mental disorder likely require medical interventions to reduce the likelihood of harm (to themselves and others) and to enable them to be productive members of society. Mental wellbeing, on the other hand, is more about your thoughts and feelings and how you cope with the ups and downs of everyday life.

The two are, of course, linked but our tendency to use them interchangeably has left many people unsure of how to handle their emotions and struggling to tell the difference between a bit of a bad day (or mood) and an issue which may require more intervention. Rejection, loneliness and difficulty have always been part of life, but the line between regular emotions and something more serious is harder for many to distinguish. We need to draw a soft line between the regular ups and downs of the life and the ups and downs that might require more support.

At one extreme, life can be full of immense and ecstatic joy, at the other, deep and dark sadness. Generally speaking, we'll spend 2.5% of our time in each of these extremes, we'll spend 25% of the time kind of happy or kind of sad and the

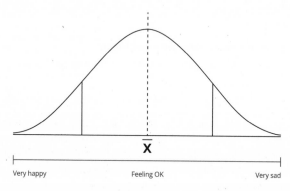

| Very happy | Feeling OK | Very sad |

How most people feel most of the time

overwhelming majority of the time – 70% – we'll be neutrally ok and fine. Obviously this is a general metaphor for life and everyone is different, but I find it a useful measure. So, in an average year, you'll have 10 days where you feel absolutely rotten, 10 days when you'll feel wonderfully joyful and the other 345 days you'll just basically get on with living your life.

All this is by way of saying that we do ourselves a disservice believing that we should be feeling happy and confident 100% of the time and that anything else is a reflection of poor mental health. For hundreds of generations and billions of people this has been true. You are awesome and unique but your life is not so vastly different from the billions of others who have walked this earth. You may have 15 days of delirious joy, you may even have 30 but you won't have 365, and that's a fact.

Everyone struggles with their mental wellbeing at some point in their lifetime because change is an inevitable part of growth, challenge an inevitable part of choice, and difficulty, rejection, loneliness and struggle are inevitable parts of life. If we pay attention to our wellbeing so we are able to understand and build resilience, we won't be held back from reaching our potential. We will be able to withstand the shocks and knocks and disruptions that are inevitably coming our way but which will inevitably make us stronger, more creative and better able to adapt to each new challenge we face.

Students and financial health

Financial wellbeing is about a person's ability to control their finances rather than being controlled by them, to set their finances in such a way that their money works for them regardless of the circumstances. Being financially resilient is at the core of this – looking after your money and not getting into difficulty over it. And this is incredibly important because money is at the core of much of our ability to care for ourselves.

Leaving home to study is often the first time any of us have been in sole charge of our finances – the money we need to live, study, eat and socialize. Historically, universities were cathedrals of learning - you came, you went to your lectures, you wrote your exams, got your qualifications and moved on. You were responsible for your learning but also for sorting out your own social life, managing your own career and fundamentally taking care of your own affairs.

More recently, however, universities have become responsible for more than just teaching their students, and "student success" has become a strategic objective of many universities and colleges.

This has included creating student service departments that incorporate careers guidance, entrepreneurship hubs, mental health and accommodation services, as well as financial services that provide everything from scholarships and financial hardship support to financial education and guidance. This is important because a holistic approach to student wellbeing is incomplete without discussing money. And a byproduct of this is that it allows young people to learn to walk the financial tightrope while there is a strong net underneath!

Understanding the challenge

Financial challenges impact mental health and wellbeing, and vice versa. By only looking at one part, we cannot see the whole picture. And this is something that extends beyond students – financial stress negatively impacts people of all ages and stages of life.

A 2018 Money Advice Service survey found that 55% of UK adults said they were worried their own mental health or wellbeing was being affected because of worrying about their finances. In addition, 22% reported being anxious, stressed, or worried about speaking to a bank and 19% tried to avoid the distress of opening bills.

The body of research around the mental health of students has grown exponentially over the last few years and there is increasing evidence to show the relationship between financial health and mental health and how that specifically impacts young people, and those in education.

- The UCAS "Spend Student Lifestyle 2020" report found that almost a fifth of students reported that financial concerns had impacted their wellbeing.
- The "Measuring Financial Anxiety" study[i] – research jointly conducted by the London School of Economics and the University of Cambridge – found that the highest levels of financial phobia are among the 16–24 age group.
- Unite Students (student accommodation provider) conducted a survey in the UK in which 41% of students reported feeling very or fairly concerned about being able to repay their loans. This figure rose to 48% among students from the lowest socio-economic group.[ii]

One thing all these statistics point to is that it is imperative that students are armed with the skills, confidence and understanding to manage their financial wellbeing despite the stress of the major life event that is moving to university. And while financial stress can impact mental wellbeing at any time in your life, if you learn some basic skills for staying financially healthy while you are a student, you can carry these with you always.

Stress and balance

Stress – we all know what it means to us but, interestingly, there is no formal medical definition of stress, and there is widespread disagreement over whether stress is the cause or the result of problems.

Stress is your body's way of responding to any kind of demand or threat. When you feel threatened, your nervous system responds by releasing a flood of stress hormones, including adrenaline and cortisol, which rouse the body for emergency action. Your heart pounds faster, muscles tighten, blood pressure rises, breath quickens, and your senses become sharper. These physical changes increase your strength and stamina, speed up your reaction time, and you go into what's known as the "fight, flight or freeze" stress response.

This is a physiological reaction and is your body's way of protecting you, having been programmed by thousands of years of evolution to keep you alive. Of course, you don't need to be chased by a lion for this carefully orchestrated and immediate survival response to kick in – a looming deadline, financial anxiety, an argument with your partner or even thinking you've lost your phone can all trigger this reaction.

Stress, when managed well, helps you to stay focused, energetic, and alert. In emergency situations, it can save your life, and it's what keeps you alert during a presentation in class and sharpens your concentration in a test or exam. When stress becomes overwhelming, however, it stops being helpful and can start causing damage to your mind and body. Over time, repeated activation of the stress response can lead to serious health problems.

The unique stress of money

Unsurprisingly a major component in chronic stress is money. One in five (21%) of UK adults told the Money Advice Service that they are drowning in debt and money worries.[iii] Indeed, many Britons have money on the mind so much that they are losing sleep – 31% reported an increase in tiredness due to lying awake at night worrying.

Money problems don't just cause you to toss and turn at night. They can create a feeling of helplessness and hopelessness, which, in turn, can create less than optimal financial outcomes, which result in more stress – a vicious financial circle that can result in what psychologists call "learned helplessness".[iv] And this feeling of helplessness has very real medical and health consequences.

So why is money at the centre of so much stress and anxiety? Because money stress is a unique type of stress. It causes psychological and physiological damage even when there isn't an impending problem. Economic instability nationally, and concerns about work, are enough to drive up stress because of the *anticipation* of a potential problem. This is why money stress can so easily turn chronic, especially for people in insecure jobs or receiving unpredictable income.

Understanding your psychological relationship to money will make managing your financial wellbeing much easier. It also enables you to better grasp the power of money but also to be more in control of your own emotions toward it. We'll look at this in more detail in Chapter 2 (see p23).

While the only way to reduce financial insecurity is to earn sufficiently, manage debts, build savings and start preparing for the future, there are some important psychological actions you can take right now to reduce the likelihood of long-term financial anxiety:

- Get more involved in and aware of your money and engage with your finances regularly. Do not stick your head in the sand hoping they will go away. Like the proverbial boogeyman under the bed, only by shining a torch on your fear can you see that in fact there is nothing to fear, or at least nothing you can't handle. Read more, learn more, treat your money the way you would any muscle – one that needs regular exercise and check-ups.

- Create a flexible plan: most people function better when they have a plan, and wise people adjust the plan when new information or circumstances come to light. Even being able to see a few weeks or month ahead will give you a feeling of control regarding your money, and with control can come confidence and action.
- Get help. It's hard to think straight in a vacuum and sometimes a second pair of eyes and someone you trust holding up a metaphoric mirror is all you need. Many people turn to family and friends for money advice, but remember there are loads of professionals, charities and others out there who can help too! See the Additional Resources section at the back of the book for some contact details.

Managing stress

It is clear that stress has both benefits and drawbacks. Learning to manage stress, and to reduce it when it is unnecessary is a key life skill. Here are some pointers on how to manage stress levels and take steps to reduce them:

- **Take time out.** It's a real cliché that stepping away from something will give you a better perspective on it. With few things is this as immediately noticeable as stress. By stepping out of, or away from, a situation you can concentrate on the real issue at hand and see through the fog of developing anxiety (your author takes long road trips to clear her mind and quieten her brain).
- **Be realistic.** Some things are stressful – and that's ok. Ray Dalio, American hedge fund manager and philanthropist, popularized the idea that you should, "embrace reality and deal with it". Dalio speaks of the importance of pragmatism and how only through pain and reflection can we truly progress. Being honest with yourself is key.

- **Own it.** Being pragmatic about what is happening and how it impacts on you is one thing, taking responsibility for it is the next level. Owning your stress allows you to better take control of your feelings and moods. It allows you to figure out whether the stress you are feeling is positive or negative. Controlling these emotions will often help you to see them more clearly and so address them more efficiently.

- **Calm down.** I know how ridiculous it sounds but triggering your relaxation response is one of the most effective ways to counter the stress response. Herbert Benson, a Harvard physician, literally wrote the book in 1975 about how to do this – *The Relaxation Response*. It includes strategies such as meditation, breathing exercises and yoga. Mindfulness is another technique that works for many. Taking just a few minutes to put strategies like these into action can have an instant positive relaxing effect.

- **Stop beating yourself up.** Negative thoughts are highly destructive and it requires discipline to remind yourself that a small mistake, poor decision or bad behaviour is far from being a permanent failure. Practice self-compassion – forgiving yourself is the hardest kind of forgiveness. In doing so you will also check in with your mental wellbeing and be better able to identify underlying feelings or emotions such as fear, sadness, worry or self-doubt, which you will then be able to address.

- **Avoid anticipating problems.** Anticipation can be wonderful (when it's for a Christmas present or waking up to go on holiday) but anticipating calamity, while very much human nature, can be unnecessarily stressful. It is important, as much as possible, to stop yourself from getting on that roller coaster before you need to. Rather than thinking of fear as an event, consider it a process and interrupt it mid-flow. This may be you telling yourself in the mirror that it is not time to worry, or projecting a different outcome to train your brain, or engaging calmly with your inner voice about the likelihood (or not) of disaster and what you might do to stave it off. Seeing yourself in control of your stress is the first (and sometimes only) step out of the stress itself.

Find your personal balance

No, you're not imagining it, the problem of stress – yours and everyone else's – is getting worse. Ralph Waldo Emerson, the American philosopher and poet said, "The purpose of life is not to be happy. It is to be useful, to be honorable, to be compassionate, to have it make some difference that you have lived and lived well."

Increasingly, many of us see work through much the same lens. It is not simply to earn a paycheck, it needs to be meaningful, impactful and provide a strong feeling of purpose in our life. This is why, in a world of rising automation and job uncertainty, we are all getting more stressed, especially in the area of our finances. The ancient Jewish text, The Ethics of the Fathers, teaches that "without bread there is no learning" – if you can't tend to your material needs, it is near impossible to pursue your higher aspirations or to feel emotional ease in doing so. In light of this changing work dynamic it is a challenge to find balance.

Enter Ikigai. This is a Japanese concept that has become popular in the last few years, and it roughly translates to "reason for being". Ikigai is a methodology of balance, and describes ways to account for all areas of your life that relate to your work and purpose. Your personal balance is found in different intersections within the diagram, and a release from financial stress can be found by finding this balance. When you work out where your passion and profession converge with the things that the world needs and is willing to pay for.

When looking for balance in your life, it is imperative that you don't forget or brush aside the financial aspect. You may or may not be highly motivated by making money, but you will always need it.

By finding this intersection, or at least striving toward it, you can lower financial stress knowing that you have taken your personal financial requirements into consideration. Chasing your passion and dreams and desires to make a dent in the world are clearer when you know you can pay your bills.

The tripod of wellbeing

Overall wellbeing is essential for a healthy and productive life and we can think of it as a tripod:

- Physical – taking good care of the body
- Emotional/mental – managing feelings, moods and consequent behaviours
- Financial – managing money to best effect for the short- and long-term

It is crucial that financial health and wellbeing is included and it also important to consider the interconnectivity of the three as they impact on each other. There is a powerful feedback loop. For example, a student with financial stress may sleep poorly, which will impact on their mental and physical health and likely lead to poor concentration in class, which can lead to lower academic performance, which can impact job prospects, which creates negative conditions for mental health, and so on.

Let's take a walk through each one in turn to explore how they all rely on each other.

Physical

It was the ancient Greeks who first promoted the importance of taking care of the body. The physician Hippocrates (460–370 BC) observed, "Eating healthily by itself will not keep a man well; he must also have physical exercise."

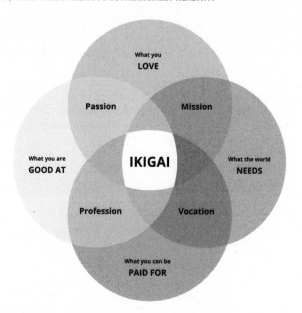

Physical perfection, in many ways, defines the civilization of ancient Greece, but it was their consideration of body and mind as inexorably linked that reverberated through the ages and changed how people consider their health and wellbeing. It was Pythagoras (the triangle guy!) who believed that body and soul should be "tuned" to each other and treated with equal care and respect.

Though all this thinking happened over 2000 years ago, their holistic approach is almost intuitive to us today. Global health organizations encourage people around the world to revisit the concept that, when it comes to our wellbeing, everything is connected and should be viewed as such.

We often see, and feel, this connectedness most clearly in our physical presence. When things are not going well in our lives the most obvious signs are physical ones. To return to our sleep example, we may suffer low-level yet persistant headaches before those close to us will notice the bags under our eyes from prolonged sleepless nights.

Our physical appearance is an early warning system for what else may be going on in our lives. And because we are essentially a closed system, our physical health will be influenced by, but also influence, our mental, emotional and financial health. We know that making wise decisions about our physical health – diet, exercise, addressing illness – leads to greater overall wellbeing.

Emotional/mental

The promotion of mental health within the broader context of health is a far more recent event. In 1893, Isaac Ray, a founder of the American Psychiatric Association, provided a definition of the term mental hygiene as "the art of preserving the mind against all incidents and influences calculated to deteriorate its qualities, impair its energies, or derange its movements". More recently, the World Health Organization (WHO) identified three central themes around mental health: first, that it is an integral part of health; second, that it is more than the absence of illness; and finally, it is intimately connected with physical health and behaviour.[v]

Promoting mental health is an integral part of the WHO. This is because of the likelihood of mental health problems intensifying negative actions, such as substance abuse and violence on the one hand, and health problems such as heart disease, depression, and anxiety on the other. Challenges with mental health may also make it more difficult to cope with external pressures such as unemployment, insufficient income and stress.

It is wise, however, to view mental health statistics with caution. Many people have heard the top line statistic that approximately 1 in 4 people in the UK will experience a problem with their mental health each year.[vi] This is troubling but should also be viewed in context. It refers to people experiencing Common Mental Disorders (CMDs), which are defined as a loss of interest and enjoyment in ordinary things and experiences being experienced "for more than one hour in a week". This includes any aches or pains, feeling tired, struggling to concentrate or feeling irritable or short-tempered or angry.

Many of these symptoms are part of the normal cycles of highs and lows that we experience as humans. Spending an hour in a week feeling annoyed at your flatmate who spilled coffee on the carpet is something we should all be able to handle without fearing for our long-term mental health. We must take care to empower our resilience by using language carefully so that we don't feed into unnecessary feelings of helplessness and powerlessness of our own emotions.

Far more troubling is the 2014 survey showing that 1 in 14 people self-harm in the UK (up by 62% from the years 2000–2014) and that there has been a 30% increase in suicide attempts compared to the same period.[vii] The mental health charity MIND concluded that this might mean that people are finding it harder to cope with mental health problems. We also know that mental health struggles are more prevalent within some groups than others and when someone experiences multiple disadvantages, challenges can be compounded and amplified.

Everyone has less-than-fabulous days – this is perfectly normal and is, in fact, a perfectly desirable part of our life. How much more do we enjoy the pleasure of sunshine after protracted periods of grey clouds! We all go through tough times and have difficult experiences – the challenge is how to deal with these. Many of the day-to-day, season-by-season difficulties we face are ones we can certainly overcome – if not alone, then certainly with help. And while physical problems can create or exacerbate mental problems, physical exercise – especially outdoors – has been shown to improve mood and is often prescribed as a remedy for low mood and depression. Also important, as we've said already, is financial health, which is the third leg of the tripod.

Financial

Research has demonstrated a clear correlation between stress about money and poor physical and psychological health. This has multiple interrelated components. On one hand, a basic financial health education can raise knowledge, confidence and skills around this subject but, on the other hand, people who are anxious about their personal finances may choose avoidance as their primary coping strategy. Avoiding any issues with your finances will only make matters worse – please don't do this.

Dealing with money is highly emotive and the most powerful weapon we have to combat any financial anxiety is to just own it. To say "this is overwhelming and stressing me out" appeals to the rational part of the brain by acknowledging the emotional part. It all helps to get rid of the monster under the bed.

I know this isn't always easy – along with sex, money is just about the most taboo topic there is. It's all too often a source of conflict, anxiety and a myriad of emotions and anxiety. Talking about money is so emotive, and carries such power, that many would rather make avoidable mistakes than ask for help.

But restricting speech and discussion only increases and amplifies confusion, anxiety and a misplaced feeling of being alone in the struggle. What a difference it would make to so many if we knew there were others struggling equally with debt, guilt, mismatched budgets. How much might speaking with others in similar situations shine a light on better habits, practices and perspectives?

A global lack of financial literacy – a subject universally called for but still only presented in a minority of classrooms, lecture halls and work places – is also a contributing factor.

The money taboo is particularly harmful to students who are likely experiencing financial challenges for the first time as they manage their income and expenditure. (There are plenty of tips on how to do this in the following chapters.) As we discussed earlier, chronic and ongoing stress that is not addressed can damage the body, physically and mentally, and paying attention to your financial health can lessen your stress in one key area at least.

Being conscious of the three parts of the tripod of wellbeing is crucial to developing strength and resilience in each of them. This, in turn, calms our anxiety and lessens our stress as we recognize that life is about progress not perfection, and everything is a journey.

Financial health and success

Defining success in any discipline depends on setting expectations. So, how do you define financial success? What you earn, and how you utilize, protect and grow that money will all play into your objectives and goals and ultimately your feelings of financial success. No pressure!

Just like in any discipline, to define your goals and objectives you need to understand the rules of the game. When it comes to your finances the biggest threat to achieving success is (i) a lack of understanding, and (ii) a lack of discipline.

A lack of understanding is perhaps the most frustrating and common threat. Not understanding the language of money and finance, or how they work, means being unable to make our money work for us. It might mean avoiding risk when you should embrace it, getting into debt when doing so runs counter to your objectives, or focusing on short-term desires instead of long-term goals.

Meanwhile, a lack of financial discipline will likely result in an inability to stick to a plan or overcome the obstacles standing between you and your financial goals. You need to be able to overcome the need for instant gratification, to build a healthy financial mindset and to cultivate a healthy ongoing relationship with money. Having great money discipline means recognizing that money is just a vehicle to get you to financial health.

Your financial health and wellbeing will depend on your ambitions, goals and timelines. This book is intended to help you better understand what it means to be financially healthy and how to apply this to your own life. And then it is up to you to determine a plan, and execute it, to ensure you can manage your finances in a way that works for you.

Hopefully, you now have a better understanding of what being financially healthy means and how it really is a key part of overall health and wellbeing. Students are at a unique juncture in life, and now that you have an idea of foundations, let's get into building on some of the specifics – especially around getting ready to transition to university and how to prepare your money for a smooth journey!

CHAPTER 2

GETTING FINANCIALLY READY
FOR FURTHER STUDY

This chapter is all about transitioning to university, and understanding where your finances fit in to this. We'll take a look at our personal responsibility toward our finances and how to get ready for this big life change. We'll also explore how it's never too early to start setting some financial goals. But first, let's talk about attitudes toward money and what might cause them.

What causes our money attitudes?

Money is very rarely just about money. It's not only about the stuff it buys and the opportunities it affords. It is often seen as the ultimate tool (or weapon) in our pursuit of contentment, success, happiness and wellbeing. And it is our attitudes around money that can seriously influence how much of it we have, how we earn it, how we spend it, how we view it and what we think of it.

Early learned experience

The Cambridge University study, "Habit Formation and Learning in Young Children" [viii] found that adult money habits are set by the age of seven and, as such, the learning, experiences and situations we encounter as young children can have a disproportionate impact on our money attitudes as adults.

So, your childhood experience of money is critical. It's perhaps unsurprising to hear that if you grow up in a more deprived household, or through an economic recession that badly impacts the family's finances, you may have a different attitude to someone raised in relative wealth or financial security. However, it might be something you've not given much thought to before. The more we look at this topic and understand it, the better informed we will be, and better able to shine a light at that monster under the bed rather than running away from it.

Religion and culture

Money, and its accumulation and use, feature in all major religious and cultural groups. Almost all highlight the need to give charity and take responsibility – personal or communal – for the poor. And some attach a great amount of guilt to money, frowning upon ostentatious shows of wealth as sinful.

Tithing – giving a set amount of your income away – is often a feature of many religions and cultures, too, and in Judaism and Islam there are also restrictions and rules around debt and the paying and receiving of interest.

Whether these attitudes and rules have been strictly observed in your own family or have just run as a subtext in the background of your life, they can play a big part in influencing your own views on money, risk and debt.

Personal characteristics

The "Psychology of Money" study – a joint study between University College London, the Open University and BBC Lab UK – found that age and gender are also, unsurprisingly, important factors.

Regarding age, younger people's time horizons are different to older people and, as such, they tend to be more motivated by the "now" and are less likely to be thinking about the future than older people – especially those closer to retirement.

Gender also plays a role and, alas, the clichés are supported by the science. The study finds that women are more prone to worry about spending and men are more likely to view money as a vehicle to freedom.

The most important personal characteristic however is neither age nor gender – it is income. As our levels of income, debt and savings change, so too do our money attitudes. As we earn more, we are more likely to take some risks, for example with our investment strategy, and are more likely to look at debt as a vehicle for wealth accumulation than a path to financial ruin.

There is no one way to develop good financial habits, but there are lots of characteristics, attitudes and behaviours we can acknowledge – cultivating the useful ones and moving away any unhelpful ones – that will enable any of us, from any background, to get smarter with our money.

The role of personal responsibility

And now for the bit no one talks about – the fact that so much of your financial health is in your own hands.

It's all too easy to follow the narrative that success is yours and failure is everyone else's. Reality check: the opposite is true! In her 2008 Harvard Commencement speech, Harry Potter author J.K. Rowling said, "There is an expiry date on blaming your parents for steering you in the wrong direction; the moment you are old enough to take the wheel, responsibility lies with you." This is an unpopular opinion but an important one. Especially when it comes to money.

In the mad adventure we call life, we are all born into different metaphorical boats. Some are strong and steady as a result of a blessed and privileged childhood, some more rickety, and some mere inflatables – difficult to steer and always at risk of sinking.

The boats we are born into are down to dumb luck – you didn't choose your parents or your circumstances but (almost) **everything else is up to you**. It is, of course, true that sometimes life's unfair and sometimes throws you curveballs. Also, for the most part, it doesn't matter.

In 2019, a survey showed there are 2,604 billionaires in the world, and that 55.8% of them are self-made. Over half the billionaires in the world made their money all by themselves.

Oprah Winfrey was born to a teenage single mother in Mississippi and often went without water and electricity; Starbucks chairman and CEO Howard Schultz speaks of "the scar and shame of being a poor kid living in government-subsidised housing"; and Warren Buffett, the greatest investor alive and fifth richest man in the world, attributes his wealth to luck, saying, "I was born in the right country at the right time."

Most of us will never be billionaires, but equally most of us need never be poor.

Most people in what we refer to as the developed world – democratic countries with a capitalist economic foundation – have the ability to meet their needs and live a good life. It is true that we can't always have what we want, and it is a universal fact that we can't have everything we want, but the overwhelming majority of us can have everything we need.

Sometimes that means reducing our spending on other things, and sometimes it means being more aggressive with our incomes and looking to earn more. It always involves taking personal responsibility for our finances. And that's what budgeting is all about.

Many people believe that being smart with money, budgeting and being self-controlled when it comes to spending means not living a good life. This is a terrible misconception and only by moving beyond it can you really start to plan for your finances.

Nobody plans to fail. But some – perhaps many – fail to plan and to acknowledge the financial challenges of being a student, and look instead for reasons and excuses to relinquish responsibility. And that is the moment of truth. Deciding who's in charge of your money (and your financial future). Taking responsibility for your money means being honest with yourself, and holding yourself to account when it comes to your finances. If you don't have any control over your money, or a plan for how to reach your goals, you haven't really taken charge of your finances.

To take control means taking budgeting seriously, understanding and being cautious with all kinds of debt, and being wary of financially high-risk behaviours, such as gambling, while also internalizing the power you have over your life and your future.

It's worth noting that many of us make lifelong friends at university, and taking a moment to think about the people you are hanging out with will lead you to develop relationships with those who have a similar view of life to you. Making new friends can be terrifying, exciting, rewarding and challenging but, in the realm of your finances, finding others who hold views that are similar to yours will more likely result in a financial situation you are happy with. And, as we saw in Chapter 1, financial wellbeing is inextricably linked with your physical and mental wellbeing too.

Transitions are hard but change is good

Going to university is filled with a myriad of firsts. Everything is new and a change from what you are used to, making the transition period quite stressful for most students. But here's the kicker – change is inevitable. Growth is by definition a change, so if you want to grow you have to learn to adapt to change, because managing, embracing and adapting to change is at the heart of success. As Dolly Parton once said, "We cannot direct the wind, but we can adjust the sails."

You'll be faced with many challenges and it's important to recognize that although it can feel overwhelming at times, it's also important to have fun and enjoy yourself as well. Some of the challenges you might face can include:

- Sudden transition to independent living
- Feelings of anxiety, nerves or being overwhelmed
- Independent study and being self-motivated
- Making new friends
- Homesickness
- Learning how to manage your time efficiently
- And, of course, managing your money

But you can do this. Think of yourself as the greatest piece of technology on the planet: you need to start as a v1 and then upgrade as you go. Experiment, iterate, improve, test, fail, try again...

While many of these things cannot be dealt with in advance, spending some time organizing your finances is something that you can do. And looking at all of your potential outgoings is a good place to start.

Assessing your costs

The cost of basic student life can vary quite a lot from city to city and even campus to campus. You'll be surprised how quickly it all adds up, especially if you are going to university, living away from home and managing money all for the first time. Individual universities usually provide an expected cost of living breakdown on their website so that you can have a general idea of how much it will cost you to live and study at your university.

Planning ahead is your best weapon in a successful transition, which is why budgeting is so important. It means you will know at any given time if you are spending more than you should or if you are actually on track. Everyone's financial experience is, of course, slightly different but there are broad categories of spending that will apply to almost all students. Let's take a look at what they involve.

Rent

By far the biggest expense for students after tuition fees is rent. In the first year at least, most students live in university accommodation, which may be more expensive on the face of it but may include utilities, food and cleaning.

Private accommodation is for more independent living. You are usually responsible for paying rent and utilities, buying and cooking your own food, taking care of your own laundry and making sure there is enough toilet paper. Not to mention wifi and a myriad of other household stuff you have to take care of.

Utilities, phone and internet bills

If you are responsible for paying for utilities (gas, electricity, water, etc.), you will need to account for these and should shop around for the best deals. If you're going to be in shared accommodation be sure that everyone is paying when, and what, they should so you don't find yourself having to pick up the whole bill. Also, be careful about whose name is on the various accounts because this can potentially negatively impact your credit score if bills are late or unpaid!

Regardless of your living arrangements, if you have a phone you'll have a phone bill. Again, make sure you are on the best deal that works for you and think twice (and three and four times) when considering whether or not to upgrade your phone. Phone companies are wise to the "show off" factor which is why new phones are released about every 18 months, causing many people to break their contract or upgrade mid-cycle.

Food and other essentials

We've heard way too many stories of people skimping on food to save money to not put it front and centre here. Food is sustenance – it's what keeps you healthy, enables you to concentrate and stay well. We've heard almost as many stories about students who don't eat enough as we do of students who eat unhealthily and too much.

Your relationship with food will of course determine how you behave toward it and so understanding yourself is crucial. Do you know how to cook? Are you vegetarian or vegan? Do you eat only what's in season? Is eating organic important to you? And of course, do you drink a lot of alcohol? These are all things to consider when planning your food budget as they will all impact on your weekly shopping bill.

Books and equipment

Different courses will have greater or lesser requirements of texts and equipment. Books for medicine can cost a fortune, fashion students need to create a line, geography students may need to do a stint abroad. All these requirements have a cost, which should be considered early. Ideally, the cost of a course shouldn't influence your decision to take it but being prepared is way better than unprepared.

Some stuff can be borrowed or bought second-hand (or cheap!) and the university will likely have offers on textbooks. Otherwise, you could try textbook swap websites and make use of the library. And if you want to go fully digital there are now numerous companies that offer subscription models allowing you unlimited online access to textbooks.

Travel costs

Day-to-day travel, especially in some of the bigger cities, can add up to a fair chunk of change, although some unis offer subsidized or even free transport. And if you are at a campus far from your family, you may need train, or plane, fare as well. There are ways to mitigate this, such as booking in advance or buying multiple tickets, but also look our for other options. Many towns are now very bike friendly, for example.

It's common sense to avoid potentially dangerous situations by calling a cab instead of, say, walking home alone late at night, but it's also a good idea to add some of these contingency costs to the transport line of your budget.

Insurance

Once you add up all the kit you might own – laptop, phone, bike, clothes, textbooks – you are looking at thousands of pounds worth of belongings. And according to a MoneySuperMarket survey, a third of undergraduates are targeted by thieves while at university. So, protecting your stuff is important. Broken laptops, lost phones, stolen bikes – these events occur so regularly that we forget to talk about how upsetting it is if they happen to you.

Much university accommodation comes with insurance included, but it's vital that you check this and remember that it's often not included in private rentals.

Tech-enabled spending

Ah technology... thou art costing me a fortune. Tech companies the world over invest fortunes into two things: making their products easy to use and addictive. As a consequence, we spend a fortune on things and we do it impulsively and without thought. We also value convenience now far more than we ever did and are willing to pay for it even if we can't afford it. So, be sure to factor in a realistic budget, and keep an eye on, the money you'll spend on (food) delivery companies, transport apps and all other tech-enabled spending that is debited straight from your account. It can be easy to lose track of this type of spending.

Subscriptions

We are a subscription generation. From Netflix to Spotify to Amazon Prime, subscriptions can costs hundreds each year. Even if the bank of mum and dad is paying for these initially, sooner or later these costs will fall to you. Then you will need to factor that into your budget, and if there are subscriptions you are paying for that you are no longer using be sure to cancel them!

Stationery and photocopying

While environmental and sustainability pressures mean the expectation to photocopy and print stuff has dropped, it can still be a significant enough cost that you should prepare for it. In some instances, it may make more sense to buy your own cheap printer (though beware the cost of ink cartridges – it's far better to sign up to a low-cost subscription model) but you are likely to be able to use subsidized or free services in your faculty, student services, library or, if you are in the UK, the student union.

Going out

Loneliness is a concern for a lot of new students, but a major component of university life is building friends, contacts, connections and networks that will last a lifetime. For many people, the friendships forged are a huge part of their looking back at uni as the greatest time of their life. You need to factor in money for this. Nights out, nights in, joining clubs and societies, attending parties; all of these things will have some sort of expense.

Obviously, there is no clear answer to, "how much will I need for this" – different people will want to do different things with different frequency, so this is "know yourself" time. If you are a real foodie or experiential instagrammer and want to do all the new things and be seen in all the cool places, chances are you'll need more money than the hikers and the old movie buffs. And there is no right or wrong here. There are only two questions: what do you want to be doing, and what can you afford? If you budget well, the two will be the same. If they aren't then you have to decide on your priorities. Remember, you can only spend your money once!

Clothes

Obviously, you'll need clothes for uni – how we dress and present ourselves is part of our identity and the image we project to the world. Just be sure that image is truly you and that you aren't going broke trying to project someone that isn't you. Luckily, the environmental and sustainability movements have impacted on people's desire for fast fashion and made us all conscious of the effect we are having on our planet. Pre-loved and vintage, shwopping and trading have become really popular among students (and the planet thanks you!).

Of course, you'll still buy stuff and when you do, remember that students can often benefit from discounts. But remember that if you weren't planning on buying something, then that 10% off isn't a discount – the 90% is what you spent! The golden rule here is, if you don't need it, don't buy it, and if you are buying it, don't pay full price!

Interest and fines

It is always better to take things back to the library, and to avoid upsetting the bank manager by going over your overdraft limit unexpectedly, but sometimes transgressions can't be helped. So, if you're absent-minded or cavalier when it comes to cash machine withdrawals, you might want to allow something in your budget for this, so you can afford it.

Being student loan ready

While considering how to spend your money gets a fair bit of airtime, how to manage, and maximize, your student loan often doesn't.

The student loan is dropped three times a year in the UK and so, three times a year you will check your account balance and see a big chunk of money. The money that lands is expected to see you through until the next instalment.*

* If you are studying outside the UK, chances are your student loan system looks different, so be sure to check how things work where you are.

For students who don't budget, and don't have a plan, this money may seem like a lot, but they will likely discover that the loan never quite stretches far enough and they often run out of money before they run out of time to spend it.

So now is the time to consider how to make best use of that money.

The first thing to understand is exactly how much money you are likely to receive. The loan will probably be your main source of income while you're at uni. It is intended to cover your living costs while you study, and is paid in instalments. There may be other pots of money available to you – bursaries, scholarships, wages, etc. – but the important thing is to know how much you have coming in. Without that everything else becomes ever more difficult.

Once you know how much is going to be coming in, I strongly urge you to open a second bank account. You will, of course, have a primary account – likely a good student account with some perks and a free overdraft – but I'm suggesting that you open a second. By having a second account you can budget more easily. Each time your receive your loan payment, transfer the full amount into your second account and pay yourself a weekly, or monthly, "salary" to live on.

Monthly payments

Budgeting a monthly (or weekly) chunk of money is far easier than budgeting three months at a time. No one budgets like that! If you are able to, set up standing orders (an automated payment method where you authorize an organisation to take the same amount, at the same time each month from your account, for example, rent) and direct debits (similar but the frequency and amount may change, for example, your phone bill) for all your bills. This is then something that you don't need to remember to do each month, and will give you regular payment amounts to work into your budget.

Check the dates on any monthly payments to make sure your timing is right and there is money in the account on the day the money comes out – being late with such payments can be expensive and can play havoc with your credit score. Many providers will be quite flexible with the due dates on your bills and you may even be able to arrange for everything to go out at the same time to minimize confusion and the possibility of getting it wrong.

This might require some planning on your part but once you are in a routine with your monthly payments, your financial life becomes much easier and your budget simpler. Getting into a monthly spending habit will also serve you well later, as most bills and many employers function according to a monthly cycle.

Setting financial goals

Antoine de Saint-Exupéry, author of the famous fable, *The Little Prince*, said, "A goal without a plan is just a wish."

It can seem counterintuitive to have financial goals as a student. After all, you have very little money and are often in some kind of debt, surrounded by others in debt. But goals are funny things and are often at their most useful when things are at their most unpredictable, because they lay out a path and a destination. So, even if you can't always walk the path, occasionally stumble, or even change direction, your goal can serve as a "north star" to give you your bearings.

Keep it simple and consider what taking control of your personal finances means to you. Start by thinking about your goals and deciding what really matters. Goals don't need to be lofty or earth-shattering when it comes to money – rather they should be simple, meaningful and manageable so that while you're studying they can support you to get the most out of your experience at uni, to get the best marks that you can and develop the best network possible.

These are the crucial objectives of your time at university. And from a financial point of view it is critical to recognize that the only way to turn income into wealth is to have an income in the first place. And the best way to get a good income is through a good job. And the first step toward achieving that is to work toward good marks while at university and build your social capital.

Social capital as a "currency" is a fairly new concept – it's a way to hone your personal and professional reputation and get ahead in your career. Building social capital means different things at different times. Here, we refer to it as building a network that might help you climb that ladder when you start out in your professional life.

What does personal success look like to you? When you look back after graduation, what will you be proud to have achieved? Will success be based on your academic achievements? Or defined by how much you have delved into subjects you are interested in? Is it about achieving the marks or will you view success as having lived independently and meeting great people and having a great time?

And what does financial success look like for you? Will it be about having saved enough money while you study to afford a car when you graduate? Or would you like to be able to take a gap year, or volunteer or start your own business? Or is your primary financial goal to graduate with manageable debt and begin saving once you have a job?

Different people have different objectives for their education and finances, and having a goal gives you something to work to and keeps you accountable to yourself – after all, that's the only accountability you can control. And don't restrict yourself entirely – add some fun to your goals or it becomes harder to stick to your plan.

Here are some examples of goals that might support your financial health, and some of the steps you could map out to help you achieve them.

Goal	Step 1	Step 2	Step 3
Save for a graduation holiday	Set a saving goal	Get a part-time job	Set aside a bit of money each paycheck – even a tiny amount – after three years it will really add up
Graduate into an awesome job	Ace exams and assignments by working smart and hard	Get the right social media channels (for example, LinkedIn) telling a great story about you for future employers	Build up your extra curriculars and apply for placements, summer programmes and graduate schemes
Build a strong personal network	Set out to meet different kinds of people who you know you can learn from (or with)	Join relevant clubs and societies – places you can learn and network in	Use social networks to connect, in a personal way, to different people in your chosen industry

CHAPTER 3

IT'S ALL ABOUT THE BUDGET

It's totally normal to feel anxious or down about money, and there are so many things to juggle when starting out at uni that it can all feel quite overwhelming. However, by mastering a few basic financial skills you can relieve a huge amount of the worry and gain a genuine feeling of control. Simply, it's all about the budget.

A straightforward spreadsheet of income and outgoings, broken down into months or even weeks, will make the biggest difference – you will always know where you stand and will hopefully avoid getting into bad debt and not suffer any nasty surprises at the end of your term, year or course.

This chapter will discuss the importance of budgeting and show you how to get started and create your own. It will also offer tips to cut spending as well as touching on some of the ways students supplement their income by earning extra money.

Budgeting – an introduction

Money issues can have an impact on academic success. Most students – as many as 80% [ix] – are worried about making ends meet at university, which is why learning how to budget properly and save money is so important. According to research carried out in 2018, more than a third of students said that financial worries had an impact on their mental health, and among students who dropped out in 2019, 18% said that it was due to money worries.[x] Creating a simple budget and following it can help combat these challenges and the impact they have on self-esteem and emotional distress.

Budgeting is the first step toward financial wellbeing. Money is finite. You need to live on less than you make and so examining your income (money coming in) and expenses (money going out) is a solid place to start. Like any journey, you need to know your starting point before you can truly begin.

Budgeting may also be the least sexy, most boring word in the English language! When you say it spreadsheets spring to mind. And the idea of tracking every penny... yawn! We can all think of more fun ways of spending our time. However, budgeting is the cornerstone of personal finance and getting it right means you can enjoy your free time with less worry. So, like much else that is a good idea but may not yield immediate fun, the best thing to do is find something that works for you and then get yourself in a habit.

It is basically just about having a plan. Having a budget doesn't mean your money will be sorted, but it means you have a plan for how to sort your money. It's a way to track money that's coming in and money that's going out so you always know where your money is going rather than wondering where it went! Having a budget means that you can be the boss of your money, the coach to your cash... It means giving every pound a job and having the discipline to ensure that your plan is being executed.

Along with the two components of a budget (income and expenses) there are three possible outcomes: having a budget that is balanced, in deficit or in surplus. A balanced budget is when the money going out and the money coming in are the same, a deficit is where you have more going out than coming in, and a surplus is where more is coming in than going out.

The best possible outcome is for your budget to be in surplus, because it means you have money left over after paying for everything, and that means you have the ability to pay off any debt, save or take up any opportunities that come your way.

The next best outcome is a balanced budget, which is when the incomings and outgoings are the same. Under the conditions of a balanced budget you don't have excess money to save, but you also aren't going into debt.

The least desirable outcome is ending up in deficit, when more is going out than coming in. A budget in deficit inevitably creates debt as the shortfall needs to be covered. And, as the debt grows, it increases the deficit since the debt needs to be serviced (paid back).

Personal budgets that are persistently in deficit can cause longer-term problems – debts can begin to snowball making them harder to service and pay off, credit scores may be impacted and people may find new debt more expensive (for example, with higher interest rates) as the sector sees that person as increasingly high risk.

But let's not get ahead of ourselves! First, let's take a look at your income and expenses and create your budget, so you can optimize your money and budget like a boss.

Your budget

To begin, I suggest the following simple steps to pool your information and get you started.

Step 1

First, gather together all your numbers around your spending. You need to know how much is going out – that means looking at your bank statements, bills and any other records of where you've been spending your money the last few months. Getting an idea of the average you're spending on stuff will help you get some clarity, and the more information you have the more accurate the picture will be. A good guesstimate will also do the job, albeit less accurately.

Step 2
Next, do the same with your income. You need to know how much is coming in – or how much you expect to have once your student loan kicks in – and you know how much you're getting in maintenance. As with your expenses, the more accurate the picture the more clear will be your position.

Step 3
You may need to divide any lump sum income across the year to give you a good estimate of what you have to play with each month.

Step 4
Now add up both your monthly income and your monthly expenses and subtract your expenses from your income. The difference will give you a starting point from which you can look at making adjustments as necessary.

Sample budget
Here are some sample figures we can use as an example to work through.

Step 1

Monthly expenses	
Rent	£418.00
Household bills	£37.00
Groceries	£100.00
Transport	£43.00
Insurance	£40.00
Going out	£46.00
Takeaways & eating out	£35.00
Phone	£16.00
Clothes & shopping	£25.00
Health & wellbeing	£20.00
Course materials	£17.00
Holidays & events	£20.00
Gifts & charity	£10.00
Subscriptions	£10.00
Debt repayment	£25.00
Total Expenses	**£862.00**

Step 2

Monthly income	
Student Loan	£614.00
Grant/bursary/scholarship	£0.00
Job	£250.00
Family/gifts	£50.00
Other income	£0.00
Total Income	£914.00

Step 3

Income Calculator

If your income fluctuates month to month or if you recieve an annual sum, you'll need to split this across the year to work out your monthly income. If your job is seasonal (or term-time only), it's a good idea to split your earnings over the entire year.

	Amount	Frequency per year	Annual total	Monthly total (Annual/12)
Student loan	£614	Monthly	£7,368	£614
Grant/bursary/ scholarship	£0	NA	NA	£0
Job	£333	9 months per year	£3,000	£250
Family/gifts	£50	Monthly	£600	£50
Savings interest	NA			
Other Income	NA			

Step 4

SUMMARY	
Money out (monthly expenses)	**£862**
Money in (monthly income)	**£914**
Income minus expenses	**£52**

Now you've seen a sample budget and have had chance to get your head around the steps, why not try drafting your own budget using the template on p78?

What's the outcome?

If it's balanced, and the two figures are equal, it means each amount of money has a job and your entire income is accounted for.

If your income is bigger than your expenses, congratulations! You can now decide how you want to spend that spare money. For many people, having more income can mean paying even more into any outstanding debt in order to clear it faster or using the money to set up an emergency fund. These might be great ways to put this spare money to work, but that is up to you. And that's the point – the surplus money is where you have power!

Sadly, a surplus is the experience of very few students who are much more likely to find themselves in a deficit. In the UK, a significant factor in many students' budget deficits has been the government's scrapping of a maintenance grant in favour of a loan which is contingent on household income.

This means that students from lower-income families may receive more money than those from middle-income families (and will owe more money as a result), but also there is an unofficial expectation that the middle-income kids will get a top-up contribution from their parents to cover any gap.

As at the time of writing, the student maintenance loan is often not enough to cover all the living expenses it is designed to cover. The Higher Education Policy Institute found that "the expected contribution for parents with just one student child can amount to over £4,500 a year".[xi] But for most parents, and especially parents with more than one child at university, this is an impossible ask.

Students whose parents are unable to plug this gap need to seek funding elsewhere – through scholarships, bursaries, grants and paid work – while also ensuring they cut expenses as much as possible, and all while keeping their physical and mental health intact!

Unsurprisingly, many students turn to debt facilities to balance their budgets (see the following chapter for more on this), but it is worth looking again at your income and expenditure first.

Adjusting your budget

The obvious thing to do if your figures aren't adding up is to cut your spending. The easiest thing to recommend is that you cut out spending any money on luxuries (the latte and avocado toast effect) but this is also pretty unpopular!

The trouble with cutting is that there are things you can't cut out completely. For example, you can reduce what you spend on housing but you can't cut it out altogether. Similarly, you can buy less expensive brands of food but you can't (and shouldn't!) stop eating, and the same applies to transport, books, joining societies and having nights out – they are all expenses that can be trimmed but not knocked down to zero. I'd simply recommend that you need to be honest with yourself about what you should spend on and what you should save on, and look at each category in your budget carefully.

The 80/20 rule

One way to figure out how to make adjustments to expenses is to use the 80/20 budgeting rule. This is an amended version of the 50/30/20 rule, which suggests an ideal division of your income into three brackets, as follows:

- 50% goes on things you need to live your life: rent, utilities, travel, basic food, clothing and grocery items.
- 30% on things you want: luxuries you could do without if you had to, such as takeouts, eating out, socializing, clothes, holidays, gym, subscriptions.
- 20% on savings and debt repayments: this can make a big difference to financial wellbeing as a regular amount set aside for this can get you out of debt more quickly and help you start to build an emergency fund or save for a deposit.

However, for university students this sort of ratio is unrealistic, especially since accommodation across the country can account for as much as 50% of your maintenance loan, but I do suggest you consider an 80/20 ratio. By spending 80% of your money on the things you need and 20% on the things you want, it will be clearer which expenses should be cut in order to keep your budget balanced and under control.

If you can manage this ratio throughout your time at university, you will be in a good position at graduation.

If you are in a persistent deficit, and no matter what you trim you are unable to balance your budget, then please make sure that you ask for help and support. There are stories of young people not buying medicine or not eating properly, keeping the heating off and a myriad of other money saving, but ultimately dangerous and destructive, actions. There is lots of help out there – see Additional Resources at the back of the book for some contact information.

Increasing your income

By definition, there is only ever so much you can cut from your budget because life costs money and there is a natural floor beyond which cutting more expenses is bad for your health. However, there are several under-explored avenues that students can look at when trying to increase income.

We have talked about the maintenance loan but this isn't the only income available to you as a student. There are millions given out each year in the form of scholarships and bursaries, which might be available to you, as well as various government allowances or benefits.

Many, if not most, students work a part-time job of some description while studying, and there is also a significant and growing group of students who are running their own businesses while at uni. In fact, student entrepreneurship has become so popular that many universities have established Entrepreneurship Hubs, brimming with money, support, mentorship and expertise.

Facebook, Reddit, Yahoo and Reddit were all started by college students, and while you might fancy yourself the next Zuckerburg, you can also start smaller with an Etsy, Ebay or Amazon business if you have a little extra time (and some artistic talent). Alternately you can freelance if you write, produce content, do graphic design, want to work in fitness, fashion or food… or almost anything else.

Today's technology means people can create digital businesses from their living room in a way never previously possible and, in many ways, the ability to create a revenue-generating side hustle has never been easier.

While balancing earning and learning can be difficult, for many students, working is not just how they cover any financial shortfall while they study, it is also a great way of developing marketable skills. To do both effectively, however, students need to be well-disciplined, have a good routine and get the balance right. After all, there is no point sacrificing the quality of your degree for a casual job. It's important to be clear about why you want a job and whether you should get one. I'd recommend only getting a part-time job while studying if...

- You genuinely need the money – always check your lifestyle decisions, such as your budgeting and debt management, first.
- It won't overload your schedule – a second job shouldn't take you away from your most important job of studying.
- You want to be your own boss someday and can get paid to do something you love while accumulating relevant experience.

And finally be mindful of the stress and pressure you might find yourself under as you seek to balance the priorities and adequately and effectively manage your time.

Types of jobs available

There are different kinds of jobs available, which I have grouped into the categories of traditional, less traditional and illegal! And, while it is not for me to judge, there is an increase in students doing the types of jobs that they wouldn't do if they felt they had the choice.

Traditional

Here are some tips regarding the most common types of paid work you can find while studying.

- Find work through your university: there are often loads of on-campus jobs available. These might be working in the library, being a guide at open days, working in a campus bar, retail outlet or for the students' union or centre. To find vacancies, keep an eye on bulletin boards around campus, on your university's social media and on job sites online.

- Hospitality and retail are the most obvious and common jobs for students and they increasingly pay the living wage. Because they are casual you may be able to arrange your shifts around your study schedule.
- Casual work, such as market research, telesales and fundraising, is commonly available.
- If possible, consider seeking out a job that will help you develop key skills for your chosen future career (if you have one). Use it as an opportunity not only to earn money but also to learn as much as you can about the sector, industry and skills and experiences that are valued. These are the best jobs because they enable you to graduate with relevant and valuable experience under your belt, not just the degree.

Less traditional

There is a worrying trend of students turning to potentially more risky ways to make money, such as adult and sex work. The fastest growing segment here is the "sugar babies". These are young women (and sometimes men) who find older wo/men who are prepared to spend lavishly on them. The couple establishes a financial agreement, which may or may not involve sex. Whatever you think of it, it's likely this method of making money is here to stay. If you are considering this option, weigh up the long-term pros and cons – and always make your personal safety your top priority.

Medical research is another less traditional way for students to earn money. There are a lot of paid clinical trials on which you can enrol but make sure you have fully evaluated any potential risks before you volunteer your body to boost your bank balance.

Illegal

There is an increase in illegal activities on campuses, such as drug dealing – which is obviously a criminal offence with severe penalties – and, more recently, money muleing, which some people are tricked into believing isn't.

Money muleing is when young people are recruited by fraudsters, via social media, and are asked to accept money into their bank account and to transfer it somewhere else, keeping a percentage of the transaction as payment. Money mules are organized by criminal gangs and the number of teenagers in the UK allowing their bank accounts to be used for this kind of activity has increased 73% since 2018 according to fraud prevention body CIFAS.

Be in no doubt, this is money laundering – it is illegal globally – and is often done at the behest of those involved in drugs, weapons trafficking and other activities with which you probably don't want to be associated.

Paying tax

And a last word about tax. A student job will likely not pay enough over the year to tip you over your personal tax allowance. This is the amount of money you can earn "tax free", which is currently £12,500 per annum in the UK, but it changes every year. If you do earn over this amount you will pay tax on every extra pound so just keep an eye on it. If you are self-employed, you will need to keep track of your own tax affairs – and probably file your own tax return. But if you are employed then likely you are on an income tax regime whereby your tax liability is deducted directly out of your pay, by your employer.

Hopefully, you now feel more confident about budgeting – which is important since budgeting is at the core of almost all other money matters. As you can see, there are different ways to budget and you understand that by setting a deliberate plan for your money you can not only organize your finances but also relieve yourself of much associated worry.

The other reason budgeting is important is what we address in the next chapter – debt. If you are spending beyond your income, then the difference between what's coming in and what's going out is funded by debt. Debt becomes inevitable under those conditions. Let's take a closer look.

CHAPTER 4

UNDERSTANDING DEBT

Now that you have a handle on the importance of budgeting, it's time to talk debt and how it affects students in particular. Without a proper understanding of debt, you can find yourself in a financial hole, which gets deeper and more stressful the longer you are in it.

In this chapter we are going to explore the fundamentals of debt, the language used and explain the key benefits, and dangers, of taking out a loan of any kind.

NB: Although much of this is applicable globally, the terms, systems and language used in this chapter relate predominantly to the UK. For country-specific resources, you can refer to the Useful Resources section at the back of the book.

What is debt?

Far too many people don't fully understand how loans work, or how debt can impact their lives. Debt is, quite simply, an IOU. It is the obligation to pay money under an agreement.

You're in **debt** when you've borrowed money (the original amount you borrow is called the capital), which needs to be repaid back later and usually with **interest** (this is the penalty or price you pay for using someone else's money). When you put money into any kind of savings account, interest is the reward you get for lending someone else your money.

The amount of interest applied is determined by the **"interest rate"**, which is calculated as a percentage of the loan. It is generally expressed as an annual percentage rate (APR) and applies to the part of the loan that is still outstanding. This is the APR advertised. It is important to note that lenders calculate interest differently, they compound the interest at different intervals (see below) and have different minimum repayments – this is something you should always check with the lender.

Compound interest

Unlike when you borrow a fiver from a friend and then give them back their fiver, when you take out a loan from a lender or bank, the interest that needs to be repaid is **compound interest**. This is so called this because interest is charged not only on the capital but also on the interest that was applied to the capital. So it's interest on interest.

And it is this compounding which makes the capital increasingly bigger. Einstein called compound interest the eighth wonder of the world but he must have been a saver because compound interest is a real double-edged sword – it's great if you're saving money (making your savings pot bigger faster), but it can be crippling if you're borrowing money.

You can't understand debt properly without also being clear on interest, because it is the interest that will determine how expensive your debt becomes to service and how long it will take you to pay off.

When we speak of **servicing a debt**, we are talking about the payment you need to make each month in order to pay the debt back within the allocated time. Usually, there is a minimum required payment to service your debt and you must pay at least this each month.

The minimum repayment on a credit card is usually about 3%, meaning that if your bill is £500 at the end of the month, the credit card company requires you to pay at least £15 as a monthly payment. If that is all you pay each month you could take significantly longer to repay the debt and, as a consequence, you end up paying back an awful lot more than you borrow.

Compound interest is the reason why so many debts become so difficult to pay off. The longer you hold them, the bigger they grow, and the more difficult it is to pay them off. Here's an example,

- **Amount borrowed:** £1,000

- **Interest:** 20% per year (the APR)

    ▪ **If repaying a 3% minimum only:**
    The debt will take 3 years and 11 months to pay off. It will cost a total of £409 in interest.

    ▪ **If repaying £50 each month:**
    The debt will take 2 years and 1 months to pay off. It will cost a total of £203 in interest.

Having explained the potential pitfalls of compound interest, it is important to point out that debt is neither absolutely good nor absolutely bad. It's a tool that can help you along in life if used responsibly and efficiently. It is overly simplistic to say you should never get into debt. It's also not true. Not all debt is the same and using debt to build wealth is one of the most common paths to financial security.

This is when debt is used responsibly with a clear plan and objective. Buying a home, building a business, investing in your education and being able to take advantage of opportunities often rest on your ability to access lines of credit when necessary.

Types of borrowing

We have become so used to people and nations being in debt that we have begun to think of debt as a normal state. So is a certain amount of debt inevitable for students? Unfortunately, for many students the answer is yes. However, there is good debt and bad debt, even for students.

Bank overdraft

Consider the interest free overdraft that so many banks offer as a part of student accounts. Although the overdraft is debt, and needs to be repaid at the end of your studies (usually it will lose its interest free status within 6–12 months of graduating), it remains one of the best debt tools available while you are studying. It ensures you have access to credit when you need it and, provided you use it well, or don't use it at all, you should be able to pay off the balance before it attracts big interest.

Payday loans

These, on the other hand, are by far the worst possible debt. And not just for students. Payday loans are short-term loans of small amounts of cash that charge exorbitant interest rates. They should be the absolute last option if you have a temporary shortfall and if you are unable to get a loan (or grant) from the university, borrow from your parents, use your overdraft – all of these would be preferable to using a payday loan.

Credit cards

Credit cards are also generally bad debt for students because although they can be useful, they carry heavy interest rates and unless you pay off the entire balance, in full, at the end of each month the interest can very quickly become uncomfortably large.

One advantage they do hold is that many credit companies now offer protection for authorized transactions online, meaning that if you make a purchase but the supplier does not deliver, you can file a dispute with the credit card company who can help resolve the situation.

Should I have a credit card at university?

The best (and only!) reason to have a credit card while at uni is to build your credit score – and you'll have plenty of time to do that once you graduate and are earning a steady income. But if you want to start early, and you are disciplined (that's the key!), if you can secure a credit card, with a tiny limit, and use it once a month and pay it off in full each month you can get a jump on your credit score. But credit card debt builds fast so you need to decide if it's worth it and if you aren't 100% comfortable about clearing the balance in full each month, you're better off waiting. Most students graduate with a negligible credit score and that's ok.

Opportunity cost

One of the most misunderstood and yet critical aspects of finance is opportunity cost. It means that for every decision you make, there are lots of other options you decide not to pursue – there are an infinite number of things to buy but you can only spend your money once. By definition, the choices we have are infinite but the decisions are binary.

Money that you spend on buying a coffee is money that you are not saving; money that you use to pay off debt is money that you are not using to save for a deposit; money that you use to buy a laptop is money that you can't use to buy a textbook.

Opportunity cost is everywhere and the right decision is not always clear. So, juggling the various financial demands of university becomes important. For example, if your objective is to develop entrepreneurial skills and there is an entrepreneurship society that costs £100 to join you may see that as money worth spending, whereas if your goal is to maximize your marks you'd not see joining that society as a good use of funds but may think differently about a £20/hour tutor. This is where the goals we spoke of earlier in the book will help you make sense of your priorities.

When faced with a financial decision, what is right for you may not be right for somebody else, and what is right for you today may not be right tomorrow and may not have been right last week. Financial decisions must be considered regarding both their immediate effect and the potential impact that they will have on the future.

Be honest with yourself

Many students arrive at university already in some kind of debt. This is not the end of the world but it does mean that an already semi-stressful start to your tertiary education journey can be that much more pressured.

If you are coming to university with debt – whether credit card, payday loan, overdraft, maintenance loan shortfall or some other debt, be sure to factor this into your financial planning. Just because you don't have enough income doesn't mean you don't have to pay your debts. Additionally, as well as the pressure, if you have too much debt you may struggle to get an overdraft, credit card or loan because of your credit rating.

It may sound obvious, but debt is a big expense, and servicing debt can take a big chunk out of your monthly budget. If you need £200 a month to service your debt then that is £200 you can't be saving or spending the way you want.

So, when looking at your money for uni, it's time to be completely honest with yourself about your financial situation. It's all too common for people to stick their fingers in their ears and ignore the amount of debt they've accrued. Or, they might have the attitude, "well, if I'm £1000 in debt, another £100 on top isn't going to make much difference is it?" and in that way they fall victim to many more problems.

Your mistakes do not define you but they do need to be addressed. A small and manageable challenge can fast become a large problem if you don't seek help even when you know you need it. If you are in debt and anxious about managing it, help is readily available and can make so much difference to the problem. It doesn't matter how you got here – whether it's because of silly spending or an out-of-your-control change in circumstances – the important thing is to get your debt under control with a debt-management plan.

Help is available

One of the little appreciated facts about university is the inordinate amount of support available. If you're struggling with money, get in touch with your university or college's finance department, and see how they might be able to help. You might have to book an appointment, or there may be regular drop-in sessions.

From student service departments full of super passionate and knowledgeable people who want to help, to student unions and welfare centres created for the express purpose of looking after you. If ever there was a place with a safety net it's university.

While cutting your spending down and becoming more frugal is a solution most of the time, there are times and situations where – no matter what you do – you can't get to the end of the month without running out of money. So, if you find you need to go into debt each month just to pay your bills, or the only way to pay for food is to use a credit card, then ask for help. Speak with a money advisor or student finance counsellor – the sooner you do it the sooner you can start to reverse your money problems.

You are not alone, and while you are unique on the planet, everything you are going through has happened before. I hope this helps you to understand that there is help available and that you should take it.

Everyone deals with personal debt at some point and now that we've taken a deep dive into it, I hope you're feeling more confident about how to manage your money, and if you have debt – how to manage and minimize it.

Debt often begins to accumulate while studying and can accumulate (potentially to worrying levels) as you enter the workforce and beyond. It's important to have a good handle on your debt and a plan for how to get rid of it.

With the basics under your belt let's start looking at the myriad of financial challenges that may face you as you enter university. Don't worry – you got this!

CHAPTER 5

COMMON PROBLEMS AND
HOW TO DEAL WITH THEM

Transitions are scary because moving from what we know to something new involves all sorts of change and, as we well know, humans hate change! Going to university is no different and you are no doubt already feeling anxious about a range of issues – from how to cope with loneliness and making new friends to learning to live on your student loan and being sure to maximize what you get from every penny.

In this chapter we are going to explore some of the most common challenges and problems and also present some hacks and tips for coping with them

Living on a low budget

The reality for most students is that they are living day-to-day with little, if any, spare cash. This in itself can cause anxiety or even depression and, indeed, this whole book is aimed at helping to manage this very situation.

How to deal with this

First and foremost, draw up a straightforward monthly budget, along the lines of the template provided (see p78), and stick to it. This really is the framework on which you make your financial plans and base your decisions.

If you can, use your budget to identify even the smallest pockets of spare money that might be liberated. You might manage to put aside a very small amount into a savings account each month – it's never too early to build in a little financial resilience to your plans. This will help you to withstand financial shocks. It means that if your laptop breaks, or an opportunity appears, you are able to deal with it without causing major financial harm.

For far too many people, unexpected, or even expected, life events trigger financial difficulties or increase their vulnerability to long-term financial difficulty. They have little or no slack to handle an unexpected event. Financial resilience is a crucial skill for students to develop. There is a wide spectrum of resilience – students have varying levels of potential savings and likely limited access to affordable credit – but taking this seriously and keeping a track of your spending may just give you the buffer you need.

And remember, if you find that you're struggling with money, the single best thing you can do is get help. No financial challenge that you are facing is unique to you and whatever you're going through there have been countless others before you and countless others to come who will struggle with the identical issue.

Sometimes it's harder to resolve it and sometimes it's easier, sometimes there is a quick solution and sometimes you have to put in more work to get out of the hole, but there is always a solution and the problem is rarely as bad as you might think. Much like a pipe leaking, the situation will get worse the longer it is left, so putting your hand up and seeking help early is the best option.

Motivate yourself with a reward

Struggling along with little money can be pretty demotivating and one way to combat this is to give yourself rewards for staying within your budget or maybe putting away that £10 per week that you'd rather spend on an extra bottle of wine or chocolate.

Motivation may be driven through a financial reward (if I get a B+ instead of a C I will treat myself with £100), a time reward (for every networking event I go to I will give myself an evening off and watch a movie), or a final objective, rewarding yourself at each milestone (I will complete this thesis and have a sneaky takeaway after every 5,000 words I write).

Rewards need not be expensive – they can cost little or even nothing at all – but they can be a great motivator for sticking to your student budget, which helps to underpin your financial health and wellbeing, which is a key component of your overall wellbeing, as we discussed in Chapter 1.

Financial anxiety

This is not a benign condition and it is pretty widespread. Researchers at Cambridge University found that 9 million people in Britain have a psychological condition they are calling 'financial phobia', whereby they become seized with anxiety and guilt when confronted with the need to manage their money.[xii] This is made all the more toxic by the fact that financial health, or a lack of it, is often overlooked in the holistic health conversation. This is, in fact, the biggest problem.

One underlying cause of financial anxiety or phobia is peer pressure. This can be described as the influence you feel from a person or group to do something you might not otherwise consider doing or even want to do. It's not uncommon to want to be part of a group and feel like you belong in a community, especially if you're new or less experienced than the people around you. But if you find yourself compelled to "keep up" with other people who seem to spend more and have more than you do, it can cause problems.

Back in the day, people may have compared themselves to neighbours or friends, but now we have the whole world of social media and reality tv to add to this. We are beset by every aspect of the lives of those living lifestyles so beyond our own that they shouldn't be the barometer against which we measure our own life. But they are.

Scrolling inanely through social media, dissecting the lavish lifestyle of celebrities, sports stars, Hollywood stars and anyone else classed as an "influencer" while bemoaning our own lives is a recipe for financial anxiety, and the bigger the circle of people against whom we compare ourselves the worse we feel about our own lot.

Being smart with your money is challenging because there is always pressure to spend by friends, family and seemingly everyone else! Saying "no" can be daunting and maybe even embarrassing. But getting into unmanageable debt is even more daunting.

How to deal with this

There are several strategies you can employ to ward off financial anxiety, or to make yourself feel better if you find yourself struggling with it.

Practise self-care

Focussing on other people distracts you from your own unique set of financial circumstances. You need to use your time and your energy to make your money management the best that it can be and, critically, live within your means, not anyone else's.

Practising self-care is a vital part of addressing all kinds of anxieties and should form part of your regular routine. Here are some self-care tips, including some specifically aimed at financial anxiety.

- Don't withdraw from life because you think you can't afford to be active or socialize. Keep seeing your friends. There are plenty of things you can do that cost next to nothing, such as meet for a coffee or participate in some sport (sports clubs are usually subsidised at uni). Taking up some form of exercise has the additional benefit of improving your mood by releasing endorphins if you're feeling low.
- If it looks like you're getting into debt, get advice on how to prioritize your debts. When people feel anxious, they sometimes avoid talking to others. Some people can lose their confidence about driving or travelling. If this starts to happen, facing up to these situations will generally make them easier.
- Be nice to yourself. This is easy to say but hard to do; people often treat their pets and friends far better than they treat themselves. Don't be hard on yourself or overtly critical. We all make mistakes, we all mess up and we all make decisions that we later regret. So, treat yourself with compassion, kindness and care. Just listen to your inner monologue and if you find you are beating yourself up about something, stop and talk to yourself as though you are talking to a dear friend.
- Keep a routine and stick to it because having structure, predictability and familiarity will give you a feeling of control and also help you feel grounded when things get tough. When life throws you an unexpected event having structure can have a hugely positive impact on your mental health.
- Get a good night's sleep. Good-quality sleep is critical for proper cognitive and behavioural functions and it just

makes you feel better. Set a realistic bedtime, ban
yourself from screens an hour before bed and don't eat
or drink coffee or alcohol in the hours leading to this.

And if you're feeling worried and this has not subsided after
a few weeks, see your doctor. Remember, you don't have to
suffer alone – there is help out there.

Take a money vs. happiness reality check

There are links between money, self-esteem and happiness.
Research finds that those with confidence and high self-
esteem approach money in terms of personal goals and
ambitions. Meanwhile those who believe they are not
worthy, or capable, of managing their money will lean into
their past failures and negative self-image, and can hinder
their financial health and growth by doing so.

In consumer-based cultures, people often believe they
will absolutely be happier with more money. A 2010 study
by researchers at Princeton University found that happiness
does indeed increase with wealth – but only to a point.[xiii] And
the benchmark above which it ceases to have impact is lower
than many think. In fact, it peaks at earning $75,000 (about
£57,000) per year.

Money quells financial fears and allows for increased
satisfaction in life, but having more won't necessarily make
you wake up happy or live your day feeling content. That has
to come from within.

Researchers from Harvard Business School and the
University at Buffalo concluded that those who base their self-
worth wholly on their possessions and perceived financial
accomplishments "can end up feeling isolated, lonely, and
lacking meaningful relationships."[xiv] Intuitively, we all know
this to be true. It's therefore important to really value your
inner happiness and guard against linking this closely with
having money as this can all too easily lead to overspending
to the detriment of their long-, and even short-term financial
goals or needs.

Give up the guilt

The first thing to acknowledge regarding personal finance is that few of us are entirely rational when it comes to money. We make well-meaning plans that we never execute, we spend when we shouldn't out of recklessness, exuberance, joy, sadness or celebration. Or we might spend too little out of guilt or regret over previous actions.

Our money behaviour can also cause shame and remorse, and this is something that happens to us all. Such feelings over our financial situation and decisions can lead to anxiety but can also paralyse us from taking action.

We feel guilty about spending money because we feel it should be saved, or that we are spending on something frivolous or because others don't have as much... Money triggers emotional responses in ways few other things do!

It's always been considered somewhat crude and vulgar to boast about wealth. And while no-one wants to sound like a show-off, a lack of ability to speak about money at all, for fear of looking or sounding dumb/ignorant/like a know-it-all, can leave young people feeling lost at sea and unable to ask for help. The lack of open discussion can make it difficult to appreciate the scale of a problem and for individuals to understand they are not alone.

An ever growing gap between rich and poor means we are constantly finding our place in the financial structure and for many students, especially those who might be first in the family to attend university, or those whose parents and perhaps even grandparents have saved and sacrificed to provide the opportunity, the burden can be almost too much to bear.

Research shows that feeling guilty is not the best way to motivate us to act better or feel better in the future. It is better to try to place your past behaviour in context. After all, how miserable are you going to make yourself? What sentence will you impose on yourself to suffer for your past money mistake?

You are more likely to forgive a friend for behaving badly than you are to forgive yourself, but I am asking you to forgive yourself for the past as you would forgive your closest friend. Create an inner 'safe space' in which to acknowledge, forgive and move beyond past money errors. Often this is the only way to move forward.

Fraud

The world is full of all kinds of people and some of them make their money by tricking others out of theirs. A fraud, or scam, is simply a dishonest or illegal plan or activity for making money. The tactics can vary – and there are loads of different types of scams out there – but the objective is always the same: to get your money.

Fraudsters are increasingly sophisticated, both online and off, and it almost feels as though once one scam is discovered another pops up. And although students are generally pretty savvy they are also seen as a soft target for fraud. This is because most students have large amounts of money arrive in their accounts a few times a year.

Falling for a scammer doesn't make you stupid – these are professional liars and thieves. They are quite simply criminals. This is why if you should fall victim to one of them, the most important thing to do is report what has happened.

How to deal with it

There are ways to recognize scams and, more importantly, protect yourself against them. Knowing what to be on the lookout for when it comes to scams is one of the best ways to protect yourself. Here are a few tips.

- An oldie but a goodie – if it sounds too good to be true, it almost always is.
- If you receive a suspicious call or text do not give the caller any personal information, and do not confirm that any information they already have about you is correct.

- If someone asks you to transfer money, or if they ask for payment in the form of gift cards, iTunes vouchers, cryptocurrency or through money transfer services such as Western Union, it is always a scam. No legitimate company, institution, government department or person will ever ask for this. Certainly they'd never ask for this by email, text or through a phone call.
- Don't click on or download anything you don't trust and don't share personal details, PIN codes or passwords. Again, no legitimate company, institution, government department or person will ask you for these.
- If you get an unsolicited email, expand the panel at the top of the message to see exactly who it has come from. You can soon tell if it's a suspicious email address. It may be similar to the company it purports to come from but if it is a scam, the email address will be filled in with random numbers, or be misspelled.
- If you are pressured to sign documents fast, or you are pushed into making a decision on the spot, be suspicious. Scammers don't want you to have time to think about it. Always be prepared to say, "no, I can't do this right now. I need to think about it". Remember, you don't owe anyone anything in situations like this.

Financial risks

There are some risky financial ventures that anyone can find themselves caught up in, but it is perhaps as students that we first come across them. The best way to deal with them is to try to avoid them altogether, but if you do find yourself in any kind of trouble in any of these areas, as we've said before, please do reach out for some help. You can go to your doctor or students' union or welfare centre, or contact any number of online services (see Additional Resources on p83).

Payday loans

These are a very expensive way to access credit and they have had their fair share of very (very!) bad press concerning countless (apparently) unscrupulous and predatory providers.

But payday lending is far from being a new phenomenon. There are writings about usury (illegally lending money at unreasonably high rates of interest) across Africa and the Middle East as early as the 5th century. In history, as in modern day, some lenders, recognizing they are often the last hope of borrowers, would resort to incredibly high interest rates and questionable practices. Fast-forward to 2006, and 250,000 people across the UK have used short term loans. By 2012, this has grown to between 7.4 and 8.2 million loans at a total borrowing amount of roughly £2.2 billion.

The main problem with high interest loans isn't just that they can be extortionate, but that far too many people find themselves in the terrible position of having no other choice. It is a truly cruel irony that those who are most likely to take out these loans are often already in financial trouble. It can be very expensive to be poor!

While a good credit score, and financial inclusion, means that accessing short-term credit can be done via credit cards or arranged overdrafts, a bad credit score, or being financially excluded (not having a bank account or access to credit facilities), means payday loans are quite simply the only available source of credit for some people. And these loans aren't just expensive, they are incredibly detrimental to wellbeing.

A 2018 report in the UK[xv] documented the health and wellbeing impact of different kinds of debt and found payday loans to have the most destructive impact on mental wellbeing, caused by distress, shame or depression. Still, despite all this, students can be drawn to this quick cash, driven by a financial culture of "buy now, worry later", which can lead such borrowing (and resultant spending) to be seen as "normal".

The best way to ward off needing a payday loan is to build up some kind of an emergency fund whereby you have easy access to sufficient amounts of funding to attend to any crisis or take advantage of a must-have opportunity.

Gambling

According to a 2014 article in *The Guardian* newspaper, it's estimated that around 127,000 young people in the UK have a gambling problem, and opportunities to get involved n gambling are increasing.

It used to be the case that to gamble you had to enter a physical location to participate in gambling, and, given age restrictions (and for some the perception of such establishments), it was harder to be parted from your money. Today, with online gambling rife, and celebrities and sport stars fronting advertising campaigns encouraging young people to bet, the opportunity to gamble is far more widespread and encouraged.

Add to that the fact that at certain times in the year students might feel "rich", such as when their student loan drops, and what is known as the "Triangle of Gambling" is complete. This is a useful metaphor – the points of the triangle are money (access to cash), time (free time, usually) and availability (access to gambling opportunities).

In addition to this, some student finance websites have entire sections dedicated to "matched betting" and how to "beat the house". Matched betting is a way to cover all of the potential outcomes of a sporting event by using free bet promotions. While this may be completely legal and is technically risk-free (as long as you know exactly what you are doing and never make mistakes) but it is feeding the nation's gambling appetite... and people's addiction to gambling. And, of course, to think of it as risk-free shows a lack of understanding for statistics. If there truly was a risk-free way to gamble, betting establishments wouldn't allow it. Gambling is big business – in 2019, the UK gambling industry was worth £14.3 billion – and the house always wins. They may be willing to lose a bit of money by giving cash back on your first bet, but that's because they know that in the long run they will easily recoup that money.

With the increased pressure on student loans, gambling can feel like an easy win. It isn't. The friend of your flatmate, whose ex-girlfriend's dad won big on the horses is an outlier – a freak winner – a highly unusual event. The risk of being struck and killed by lightning is one person in 19 million while the chance of winning lotto is 1 in 45 million. That means you are more than twice as likely to get struck by lighting as you are to win the lotto. These odds are not in your favour, they never are. Just say no!

Gambling is as addictive as smoking – if you can avoid it, all the more better for your wellbeing (and your pocket!). And if you find yourself in trouble with gambling, please seek help (see p87).

Trading

With the advent of easy trading apps – bringing frictionless trading and fractional buying to the masses – the number of young people trading in the stock market has skyrocketed. These apps have seen a flood of new clients: young and inexperienced people jumping at the opportunity to get into global stock markets.

These apps offer "commission-free" trading, a fun and addictive mobile experience and a heavily gamified user interface to encourage regular trading and a "candy crush" level of excitement and engagement. Companies tell novices that "it is different this time" and, as happens every time something seems too good to be true, it is, and money is lost.

Trading is slowly becoming the "new gambling" for students and it is becoming more common for students to consider trading their way out of student debt. But trading is not investing and it is not a game. Nor is it easy and there are no professional traders who always make money. Trading in this manner is far more closely related to gambling than it is to investing and, with such high risk and typically a steep learning curve in which you could lose all your money and possibly even more, it is best given a wide berth until you are able to trade with money you can afford to lose forever without losing the roof over your head.

Drugs and alcohol

We don't want to be judgey, and we know that university is a time of exploration and experimentation, which can involve alcohol and drugs. We also know that the use (and certainly prolonged use) of both can have negative long-term implications. However, really, it's more about the money for us. Cash-strapped students have historically shelled out considerable sums on drugs and alcohol, and while we all want students to have an amazing uni experience, we would love for that experience to not put you into lifelong debt!

There is peer pressure at university to do all sorts of things and it isn't for us to tell you what to do, or how to do it, so be careful, be safe (physically and mentally), have trusted support around you and most importantly don't use if you don't want to. Having the strength of character to say "no" takes guts, but it can also make you feel stronger in yourself. And being calm, explaining your reasons for not wanting to do something, may make you feel more confident and gain the respect of your peers – you may even give others the strength and courage to say "no" too.

Many people face financial difficulties at some point in their life – and at uni there is plenty of support, which means you needn't go through these challenges alone. The key is to acknowledge it, face it and get help if you need it. By doing so, not only will you deal with the problem in hand, but you'll also help build up and nurture some vital financial resilience. We learn by our mistakes, and this really is as true in the realm of financial health as in other areas of life.

CHAPTER 6

FINAL WORDS

No journey would be complete without talking about what happens at the end. University is a wonderful time – financial stress and strain aside, many believe it to be some of the best years of their life – but with all transitions there are challenges as we bridge from one chapter to the next.

If you thought money at uni was confusing, just wait until you leave because your financial life is about to get both more complicated and, hopefully, more exciting once you graduate and especially once you get a job.

Hopefully, this job will pay you a sufficiently high salary that you will need to start paying tax and, depending on your salary and country of residence, you will also likely be expected to begin repaying your student loan, as well as any overdraft facilities you had while you were studying.

Once you start earning (earlier if possible) you should look at putting together a financial plan. Getting into a habit of setting goals, minding your money, making adjustments and building your personal wealth is really the only way to lay smart foundations for your financial future.

As we come to end of this journey there are three truisms to consider:

- **Don't build your castle on the sand**
  A solid financial foundation will stand the test of time and the biggest barrier and greatest danger is debt. As we

have discussed, debt is just a vehicle – when used wisely it can accelerate your journeys, when used badly it can ensnare you in a bad cycle that is hard to escape.

- **Live within your means**
  Budgeting is key - it is a necessary (but not sufficient) instrument in your journey toward financial wellbeing. Spending more than you can afford is the fastest way into debt and spending less is the fastest journey toward personal wealth. Both journeys are hard so decide which one is worth the work.
- **Start small, finish big**
  In the journey toward financial security you have two assets – time and treasure. While you're a student you have quite a lot of time but not a lot of money. When you graduate, you will hopefully get a great first job, and then as you progress in your career, you will likely have increasing amounts of money and decreasing amounts of time. If you develop and nurture good habits when you first start looking after your finances, you will the reap rewards later on.

Finally, I know things may seem a bit hard at the moment. We have faced and may continue to face pandemics, political uncertainty and global upheaval. The planet is sick and our politics are broken. Our societies are unequal and young people struggle against feeling helpless in the face of huge existential problems. And, amid all of this, you are trying to understand how to best prepare yourself financially for being a student and beyond.

Some people may even tell you not to even bother with higher education – after all, who knows what the world will look like when you graduate, what kinds of jobs will be available or whether you'll be able to get one of them. It's scary and overwhelming and a little bit terrifying.

But here's the thing. Fear is part of growth and growth is critical to life and things are never as terrible as they would appear. You know that while the world is upside down it's also yours for the taking. Life may not be fair but you can make a huge dent in it. You don't know what comes next, but know it will be awesome.

You may not know what the path will bring – you can't see that far ahead – but you know the view at the end will be worth the journey. For now, you are standing in the dark, on a dirt road, maybe surrounded by supportive family and friends, maybe on your own. Either way, the path is yours and yours alone.

All you need is a map and a torch to find the next junction. Because at that junction there are some streetlights, and likely more people like you so it will be easier to navigate. And the junction after that is the freeway, scary and faster moving, but full of opportunities that will take you anywhere you want to go. All you need is a torch to light the way, and a map to guide you.

You are the torch – I hope we can be your map.

Budget template

MONEY IN	SEP	OCT	NOV	DEC	JAN
Student loan					
Grant/bursary/scholarship					
Job					
Family/gifts					
Savings interest					
Other Income					
Other Income					
TOTAL INCOME					

MONEY OUT	SEP	OCT	NOV	DEC	JAN
Rent					
Household bills					
Groceries					
Transport					
Insurance					
Going out					
Takeaways & eating out					
Phone					
Clothes & shopping					
Health & wellbeing					
Course materials					
Holidays & events					
Gifts & charity					
Subscriptions					
Debt repayment					
Other					
TOTAL EXPENSES					

SUMMARY	SEP	OCT	NOV	DEC	JAN
Income minus expenses					
Starting balance for the month					
Predicted ending balance					
Actual ending balance					

FEB	MAR	APR	MAY	JUN	JUL	AUG	TOTALS

FEB	MAR	APR	MAY	JUN	JUL	AUG	TOTALS

FEB	MAR	APR	MAY	JUN	JUL	AUG	TOTALS

ACKNOWLEDGEMENTS

Steve Jobs said, "Great things in business are never done by one person; they're done by a team of people" and that's certainly the truth of building Blackbullion. It is only by adopting my dream as their own that we have come so far and impacted so many. So here's to you Ola, Mark, Danielle, Annie, Vova, Tudor, Migle, Rosie, Irene, Ben and Lexi. Also to Stanley and Jeremy for your ongoing counsel and never-ending support.

ADDITIONAL RESOURCES

HELP WITH DEBT

UK
- Stepchange (0800 138 1111) – www.stepchange.org
- National Debtline (0808 808 4000) – www.nationaldebtline.org
- Debt Advice Foundation – www.debtadvicefoundation.org
- Debt Support Trust – www.debtsupporttrust.org.uk

Australia
- National Debt Helpline – Free financial counselling – www.ndh.org.au
- Dealing with debt – Australian Financial Security Authority – www.afsa.gov.au
- National Debt Helpline – Financial Rights Legal Centre – www.financialrights.org.au

USA
- Debt Help Organization – www.debt.org
- Nonprofit Free Credit and Debt Advice (NFCC) – www.nfcc.org

GENERAL FINANCIAL SUPPORT AND ASSISTANCE

UK
- Speak to student services on your campus

- The Citizens Advice Bureau is a good place to get information about benefits, how to deal with debt and almost anything money related – www.citizensadvice.org.uk
- All kinds of financial support – www.moneyadviceservice.org.uk

Australia

- www.moneysmart.gov.au/managing-debt/urgent-help-with-money
- The Australian Banking Association difficulty teams – www.ausbanking.org.au/for-customers/financial-difficulty/teams
- Financial counsellors – www.afsa.gov.au/insolvency/cant-pay-my-debts/where-find-help

USA

- Government program that provides financial help for individuals and organizations – www.usa.gov/benefits-grants-loans

HELP WITH MENTAL HEALTH

UK

- See your doctor
- Samaritans (08457 90 90 90) for confidential, non-judgmental emotional support – www.samaritans.org
- HelpGuide – mental health and wellness support – www.helpguide.org

Australia

- HelpGuide – mental health and wellness support – www.helpguide.org
- Mental Health Contact Lifeline for support – www.health.gov.au/health-topics/mental-health

- Mental Health information and support – www.beyondblue.org.au
- ReachOut, Australia's leading online mental health organisation for young people and their parents – www.about.au.reachout.com

USA

- HelpGuide – mental health and wellness support – www.helpguide.org
- The Substance Abuse and Mental Health Services Administrations (SAMHSA) – for people struggling with mental health conditions, substance use disorders, or both – www.samhsa.gov/find-help/national-helpline

SUICIDE SUPPORT

UK

- Samaritans (08457 90 90 90) for confidential, non-judgmental emotional support – www.samaritans.org
- PAPYRUS is the national charity dedicated to the prevention of young suicide – www.papyrus-uk.org
- Supportline – confidential emotional support for those who are isolated, at risk, vulnerable and victims of any form of abuse www.supportline.org.uk

Australia

- Lifeline Australia – www.lifeline.org.au
- Mental Health Contact Lifeline for support – www.health.gov.au/health-topics/mental-health
- Mental Health information and support – www.beyondblue.org.au

USA

- National Suicide Prevention Lifeline – www.suicidepreventionlifeline.org

- The Trevor Project offers crisis intervention and suicide prevention to LGBTQ youth – www.thetrevorproject.org

HELP WITH SCAMS

UK
- The Citizens Advice Bureau – www.citizensadvice.org.uk
- Action Fraud 0300 123 2040

Australia
- Scamwatch provides information to consumers and small businesses about how to recognise, avoid and report scams – www.scamwatch.gov.au
- ReportCyber (formerly ACORN) is the place to report cybercrimes – www.cyber.gov.au/acsc/report

USA
- Report Scams and Fraud – www.usa.gov/stop-scams-frauds
- Internet Crime Complaint Center (IC3) – www.ic3.gov

HELP WITH ALCOHOL OR DRUGS

UK
- See your doctor
- Drinkaware – www.drinkaware.co.uk
- Alcoholics Anonymous – www.alcoholics-anonymous.org.uk
- Talk To Frank (www.talktofrank.com) or 0300 123 6600

Australia
- National Alcohol and Other Drug Hotline – www.health.gov.au/contacts/national-alcohol-and-other-drug-hotline-contact
- Australian Government information about illicit drugs and campaign resources – www.campaigns.health.gov.au/drughelp

- Kids Helpline (for young people aged between 5–25 years of age) – www.kidshelpline.com.au

USA

- The Substance Abuse and Mental Health Services Administrations (SAMHSA) – for people struggling with mental health conditions, substance use disorders, or both – www.samhsa.gov/find-help/national-helpline

HELP WITH GAMBLING

UK

- Gamcare – National Gambling Helpline (0808 8020 133) – www.gamcare.org.uk
- www.begambleaware.org
- www.gamblersanonymous.org.uk

Australia

- Gambling Help Online – Support for anyone affected by gambling – www.gamblinghelponline.org.au
- Lifeline Australia – www.lifeline.org.au

USA

- Check support in your state – www.therecoveryvillage.com/process-addiction/compulsive-gambling/related/gambling-hotlines
- USA – The Consumer Affairs Debt Consolidation – www.gamblingtherapy.org
- National Problem Gambling Helpline – www.ncpgambling.org/help-treatment/national-helpline-1-800-522-4700/

REFERENCES

Chapter 1

- i **Gilla Shapiro** [The Princess Margaret Hospital] and Brendan Burchell [University of Cambridge] (2012) Measuring Financial Anxiety. Retrieved from: www.researchgate.net/publication/254734180_Measuring_Financial_Anxiety (accessed 07.09.2020)

- ii **Unite Students** (2016) 'Student Resilience: Unite Students Insight Report 2016'. Retrieved from: www.unitestudents.com/about-us/insightreport (accessed 08.09.2020)

- iii **Money Advice Service** (2017) Retrieved from: www.moneyadviceservice.org.uk/en/corporate/money-on-the-mind-a-nation-feeling-the-cost (accessed 03.10.2020)

- iv **PositivePsychology.com** (2020) Retrieved from: www.positivepsychology.com/learned-helplessness-seligman-theory-depression-cure (accessed 03.10.2020)

- v **World Health Organisation** (2004) Retrieved from: www.who.int/mental_health/evidence/en/promoting_mhh.pdf (accessed 03.10.2020)

- vi **National Health Service** (2007) Retrieved from: https://files.digital.nhs.uk/publicationimport/pub02xxx/pub02931/adul-psyc-morb-res-hou-sur-eng-2007-apx.pdf (accessed 03.10.2020)

- vii **Mind** (2020) Retrieved from: www.mind.org.uk/information-support/types-of-mental-health-problems/self-harm (accessed 08.09.2020)

Chapter 2

- viii **Money Advice Service** (2013) Retrieved from: https://mascdn.azureedge.net/cms/the-money-advice-service-habit-formation-and-learning-in-young-children-may2013.pdf (accessed 05.09.2020)

Chapter 3

- ix **Save the Student** (2019) Retrieved from: www.savethestudent.org/money/student-money-survey-2019.html (accessed 08.10.2020)
- x ibid.
- xi **Higher Education Policy Institute** (2018) Retrieved from: www.hepi.ac.uk/wp-content/uploads/2018/04 HEPI-Submission-to-the-Post-18-Review.pdf (accessed 01.10.2020)

Chapter 5

- xii **Daily Mail** (2003) Retrieved from: www.dailymail.co.uk/news/article-156764/Nine-million-Brits-suffer-financial-phobia.html
- xiii **The Proceedings of the National Academy of Sciences** (2010) Retrieved from: www.pnas.org/content/107/38/16489.full (accessed 31.08.2020)
- xiv **SAGE Journals** (2020) Retrieved from: https://journals.sagepub.com/doi/10.1177/0146167220910872 (accessed 31.08.2020)
- xv **Royal Society for Public Health** (RSPH) (2018) Retrieved from: www.rsph.org.uk/about-us/news/payday-loans-named-unhealthiest-form-of-credit.html (accessed 07.09.2020)

TriggerHub.org is one of the most elite and scientifically proven forms of mental health intervention

Trigger Publishing is the leading independent mental health and wellbeing publisher in the UK and US. Our collection of bibliotherapeutic books and the power of lived experience changes lives forever. Our courageous authors' lived experiences and the power of their stories are scientifically endorsed by independent federal, state and privately funded research in the US. These stories are intrinsic elements in reducing stigma, making those with poor mental health feel less alone, giving them the privacy they need to heal, ensuring they are guided by the essential steps to kick-start their own journeys to recovery, and providing hope and inspiration when they need it most.

Clinical and scientific research conducted by assistant professor Dr Kristin Kosyluk and her highly acclaimed team in the Department of Mental Health Law & Policy at the University of South Florida (USF), as well as complementary research by her peers across the US, has independently verified the power of lived experience as a core component in achieving mental health prosperity. Their findings categorically confirm lived experience as a leading method in treating those struggling with poor mental health by significantly reducing stigma and the time it takes for them to seek help, self-help or signposting if they are struggling.

Delivered through TriggerHub, our unique online portal and smartphone app, we make our library of bibliotherapeutic titles and other vital resources accessible to individuals and organizations anywhere, at any time and with complete privacy, a crucial element of recovery. As such, TriggerHub is the primary recommendation across the UK and US for the delivery of lived experiences.